Think Metric!

| 1 | 2 | 3 | 4 | 5 | 6 | 7 | 8 | 9 | 10 |

BY THE AUTHOR

The Christmas Sky

Experiments in Sky Watching

Man in Space to the Moon

The Mystery of Stonehenge

Pieces of Another World:
The Story of Moon Rocks

Think Metric!

Think Metric!

BY FRANKLYN M. BRANLEY

illustrated by Graham Booth

Thomas Y. Crowell Company
New York

Manufactured in the United States of America

4   5   6   7   8   9   10

Library of Congress Cataloging in Publication Data

Branley, Franklyn Mansfield
Think metric!

SUMMARY: Describes how accurate standards of measurements were determined for time, length and width,
volume, temperature, and weight with emphasis on the advantages of the metric system.
1. Metric system—Juvenile literature.
[1. Measuring] I. Booth, Graham, illus.
II. Title.
[QC91.B8]   389'.152   72-78279
ISBN 0-690-81861-0
ISBN 0-690-81862-9 (lib. bdg.)

Think Metric!

It is hard to imagine a world without accurate ways of measurement. We must measure time; the length and width of things; the volume of containers—how much they will hold; the temperatures of gases, liquids, and solids; and the weight of objects.

9

We measure, so

A house that a carpenter builds looks like a
    house,
New parts for cars fit into old cars,
Men can set out on space journeys and arrive
    at the right place at the right time,
Buyers can order cloth or oil or alcohol or syrup
    and get exactly the amount they ordered,
You can order clothes to fit,
People can buy exact amounts of food, gaso-
    line, wallpaper or rubies or diamonds,
Fudge and other candy will harden properly.

In the olden days, a thousand and more years before Columbus came to America, every monarch had
his own way of measuring things. The length of the
king's foot was the unit for measuring length. The
jousting field would be 300 feet long—300 of the king's
feet. Another king might say a foot would be the length
of four palms—the width of sixteen fingers. (You'd
think such a unit would be called four palms, or something like that, but this was one early foot unit.)

In a similar fashion, the monarch might proclaim the
unit for measuring liquids as the amount of wine that
was held in his favorite cup. As long as the king lived,
when milk was bought or sold in the kingdom, or wine
or beer, the cup would be the unit of measure—the
king's favorite wine cup. But new standards of

3

measurement might come with the crowning of a new king.

Other early units of measurement were obtained in a similar random fashion. The inch was the length of the last bone of a man's thumb. A cubit was the distance from a man's elbow (probably the elbow of the king at the time) to the end of his middle finger. Sometimes the cubit was measured as six palms.

A yard in England was declared to be the distance from the tip of King Edgar's nose to the tip of his middle finger, when his arm was stretched out. Edgar was king of the English in the latter part of the tenth century.

A fathom, used for measuring depth of water, was the length of a Viking's outstretched arms from fingertip to fingertip. Vikings were the mariners of those days.

To measure land the acre was used. It was the amount of land a pair of oxen could plow in one day. This could vary a great deal. Much more light, dry soil could be plowed than could heavy, damp soil. Also, young, energetic oxen could plow much more land than could oxen that were old, tired, and slow moving.

Another unit of land measure used in old days was the hide. This was the amount of land that a pair of oxen could plow in one year. This was around 120 acres, but it also varied a great deal: not all oxen were equally strong, some fields were easier to plow than others, weather varied from place to place.

Several hundred years ago in Germany the length of the rute, or the rod, or pole, or perch (it was called by various names), was determined one Sunday morning, as decreed by the local monarch. As people left church services sixteen men were selected. They stood toe-to-heel, toe-to-heel, and the combined length of their feet was measured. This was the standard. Forty rods became the furlong, and eight furlongs was one mile.

The mile was determined in other ways, too. One was established by Roman legionnaires when they stepped off 1,000 paces—about 1,618 yards then.

Units of measurement based upon the human body were convenient to use. The cubit (elbow to fingertip) was a length always at hand. It was useful for knotting the cords used to measure greater lengths. When reeling in a line, the convenient way to store and measure it was in cubits (roughly). Sailors do this even today, wrapping the line around their elbow and in the valley between the thumb and first finger.

To measure the weight of precious metals, or the weight of a pig or a lamb, each merchant carried his own scale and his own weights. They varied from person to person, so that one man's pound was heavier than another's.

There was no way of measuring temperature. One knew whether something was hotter or colder than

something else; he knew he could not drink boiling tea and he knew milk would freeze solid. But he did not know the temperature of the tea or the milk. No system of temperature measurement had been invented.

When shaping wood to fit a given space, the first knuckle and the palm (width of four fingers) gave rough measures, but there is a wide variation in the width of men's fingers.

7

Also, when a new king came along he would often change the measuring units. A person had to know if the wine he was buying, or the cloth or spices, was being measured by the system of the first king or the second king.

Systems of measurement were different from one region to another. A trader had to know if measurements were based on the system used in his country, or the country where the wine, grain, and spices were grown.

A trader from one country might offer salt in a foreign country at so much money per cup. But the size of the cup he used to measure salt might be much smaller than that used in the foreign country. The buyer would have to consider the price and the size of the cup to find whether or not he was getting a bargain.

As time passed, transportation and communication became better and better. When people in one region or country began to trade with people from other countries, variations in measuring length, volume, and the weight of objects became serious barriers to commerce: new ways of measurement had to be found.

There was also a growing need for precision. The first knuckle of a man's hand served to make a rough measurement. But when wood pieces had to be fitted together or matched for manufacturing a gear or some other part of a machine, such measurements were not adequate. Too much trial and error cutting and sanding were needed. Metal parts were more of a problem. When a new wheel had to be fitted to an old axle, the sizes had to be measured accurately. If the wheel hub was too big, it was a long and hard job to make it fit the axle.

People needed better systems of measuring length and width, of weighing, and of determining units for measuring liquids, grains, apples, potatoes, and the temperature of things. They needed better measurements so trade could flourish and so products could be made far from where they were to be used—with assurance that the parts would fit.

About a thousand years ago some attempts were made to improve measuring procedures. Instead of using a king's foot, which varied from king to king, to measure distance, it was decided that a foot would be the length of thirty-six barleycorns laid end to end. The kernels of barley were to be dry and round, and taken from the middle of the ear.

Such a standard was a bit better than the width of one's fingers, or the length of one's knuckle. But it was not much better; the sizes of kernels of corn varied from ear to ear and from season to season.

Standards of various kinds—some more precise than others—for measuring volume, temperature, and the weight of things were established from time to time as decades and centuries passed by. For example, in the thirteenth century Henry VII, the German king, decreed that the bushel would be used for measuring grain. This was the Winchester bushel, which was a cylinder roughly 18 1/2 inches high and 8 inches in diameter. But the inch varied, and so of course did the bushel.

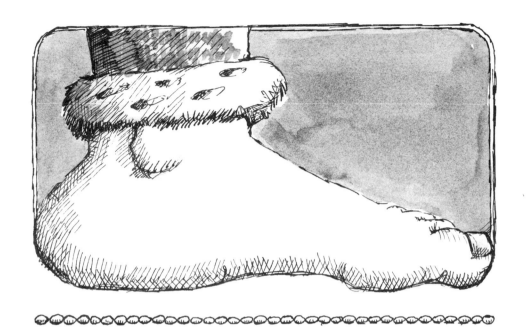

In the sixteenth century officials of Elizabeth I of England went about setting a standard for finding the weight of objects. (Actually they were seeking a standard for the mass of objects. In everyday life we use the term *weight,* even though technically we mean *mass.* Mass is the actual amount of material something contains. Weight is a measure of the force of gravity exerted upon the object. Weight changes as gravity changes—from the earth to the moon, for example. Mass does not change: it remains the same, no matter where you are.) The officials established the hundredweight (actually 112 pounds), which is still used in England. The standard for the hundredweight is a cube of metal which is presently in the Tower of London. When people wish to check their measuring devices, that cube of metal, the standard, guides them.

In the eighteenth century Gabriel D. Fahrenheit (1686–1736), a German scientist who spent much of his life in England, invented a system for making accurate measurements of temperatures. In 1714, when he introduced the system, he believed the lowest temperature that could ever be reached was the temperature of a mixture of ice and salt. Fahrenheit immersed the end of his thermometer, a thin glass tube filled with mercury very much like today's thermometers, in such a mixture. The mercury fell steadily. When it would go no lower, Fahrenheit marked the thermometer, and called that point 0°. He thought nothing could be colder.

There are many stories about how Fahrenheit arrived at other fixed points in his thermometer. One relates that he put the end of the thermometer in his mouth (or that of an associate) and put a mark on the glass when the mercury stopped rising. He called this point 100° (we know today that it is 98.6° on the F. scale). The space on the thermometer between 0° and 100° was divided evenly into degrees. When the thermometer was put into freezing water, the mercury stood at 32°. Carrying the same scaling beyond 100°, Fahrenheit found that the mercury stood at 212° when the thermometer was put into boiling water.

Progress in standardizing all measurements advanced slowly. But by the beginning of the nineteenth century England had set standards, most of which were followed by the United States. The English used the yard for measuring length and area, the gallon for measuring liquids, and the pound for measuring weight.

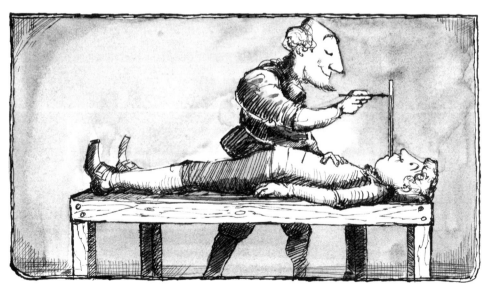

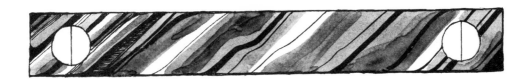

The yard was the distance between two fine lines engraved on gold studs that were sunk into a bar of bronze and kept in the jewel tower at Westminster in London, England. Metal expands when it gets warm and contracts when it cools. To be sure that the bar was no longer or shorter than it was when the lines were scribed in the gold studs, the temperature at the time of measurement had to be the same as the temperature when the marks were made; the temperature had to be 62° F. Manufacturers of rulers and yardsticks made their products as close as they could to the exact length of the standard yard. The foot (1/3 of a yard) and the inch (1/12 of a foot) became the standard units for shorter lengths. A mile became 1,760 yards, or 5,280 feet. Area was measured in square inches, feet, or yards. An acre was 43,560 square feet, and a square mile figured out to be 640 acres.

The pound was to be the mass, or weight at sea level, of a cylinder of pure platinum 1.35 inches high and 1.15 inches in diameter. For smaller masses the ounce (1/16 of a pound) became the standard.

The gallon was the volume of 10 pounds of water. The water must be pure. Also, the water had to be at a temperature of 62° F. That's because water expands or contracts as its temperature varies.

In Britain the gallon was used for measuring solids such as berries, cherries, grain, and mushrooms, as well as liquids. For measuring smaller volumes the quart (1/4 of a gallon), the pint (1/2 of a quart), the

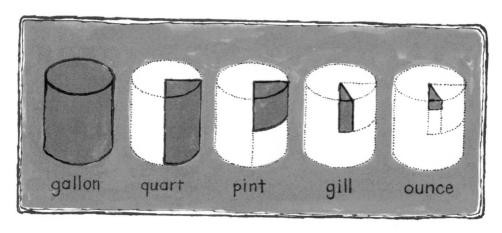

gallon   quart   pint   gill   ounce

gill (1/4 of a pint), and the ounce (1/5 of a gill) were used.

England had standards for measuring distance, area, weight, liquids—just about everything. When people had salt to sell, a cup was a cup and a pound was a pound; a bushel of wheat was always the same amount, and a thousand square yards of land was the same amount in one town as another. In every country where the system was used people understood the meaning of a hundred pounds of potatoes or three hundred gallons of kerosene or a bushel of apples. There were still a few differences from country to country, but now people could trade back and forth more easily. Also, they could manufacture parts for engines—gears, wheels, axles, any part at all—and know the parts would fit exactly. A man in America could order from England a cylinder for his broken-down steam engine and know that when it arrived the

part would fit and the steam engine would work again.

This system of measurement was changed here and there during the nineteenth century and it was made more and more precise and reliable. It was called the English system and was used in many parts of the world, including the United States. The system worked, but it was (and is) awkward. For example: An inch is 1/12 of a foot, a foot is 1/3 of a yard, and 5 1/2 yards make a rod (often called a perch or a pole). Forty square perches equal 1/4 of an acre (or 10,890 square feet). In a square mile there are 640 acres.

Inches, feet, yards, and rods just don't seem to be

related at all. It is hard to find reasons for the various units. Perhaps people were trying to retain the units they had been used to. The inch is somewhat like the "first thumb bone" unit; the foot is somewhat like the length of a grown man's foot; and the yard is somewhat like the distance from a man's nose to the tip of his middle finger. We still use these measures to get a rough idea of distance. Your mother gets some idea of the length of fabrics by measuring with her arm, and drivers measure distance between a parked car and a hydrant by "pacing" it off. The rod, perch, or pole was probably based upon the length of a given number of a man's strides, which is a convenient way to mark off land. We still measure land by strides to get rough measures.

The English system is also awkward when measuring volume and liquids. The problem is that there is no standard relationship among the units. For example, in measuring liquids, 16 drams make an ounce, 4 gills make a pint, 2 pints make a quart, 4 quarts make 1 gallon. If you were measuring molasses, 31 1/2 gallons

would make a barrel. But if you were dealing in wine, you would use a hogshead, and 63 gallons make 1 hogshead.

In the English system it is difficult to change gallons and quarts to pints, ounces, or drams. A person has to remember how many of one unit there are in another. But this was done, and different countries used the same system. Trade flourished back and forth between England and the United States, and few problems of measurement came up because both countries—and many more around the world—understood one another.

But, as the English system of measurement was developing, other systems were evolving in other parts of the world.

From time to time scientists have suggested that measurement should be based upon some reasonable standard. The length of a pendulum that takes one second to swing back and forth at the equator was one idea for the length standard. In the United States Thomas Jefferson said we should develop a new scientific system of measurement, but nothing came of his proposal.

In 1670 Gabriel Mouton, vicar of St. Paul's Church in Lyons, France, proposed that one minute of arc of a great circle of the earth be used as the basis for establishing a standard unit of length. A great circle is any circumference of the earth, the plane of which goes through the center of the earth. The equator is a great circle, so also are the meridians that run from pole to pole. There are 90 degrees of arc from the equator to a pole, and each degree is divided into 60 minutes. The unit Mouton suggested was the length of 1 minute of arc.

Apparently the unit was unworkable, or the French people were not ready to change their old systems of measurement, which had grown in much the same haphazard fashion as had the English systems. We do know that the vicar Mouton's suggestion was put aside.

Some hundred and twenty years later, in 1791, the French Academy of Sciences presented a new system of measurement, the metric system, to the French government. It took more than half a century for the people to accept the plan. But they did accept it finally. Not only the French people, but a large part of the people of the entire world had accepted the system by the latter half of the nineteenth century. These are the standards that were suggested by the French scientists: The basic unit was to be the meter—one ten-millionth (1/10,000,000) of the distance from the equator to a pole. (Actually this meter was quite similar to Mouton's suggestion made more than a hundred years earlier.) To determine the length of the meter, measurements were made along a meridian running from Dunkirk, in France, to Montjuich, a town near Barcelona, Spain. The units for larger or smaller measurements were all to be multiples of ten of the standard unit.

Different names were given to each of these units. The word *meter* is derived from a Greek word meaning "to measure." The names for the larger or smaller units simply add a Latin or Greek prefix to the word for the basic unit. Thus the meter is the standard for length, but the kilometer (*kilo-* means "thousand") is the unit for larger distances, and the centimeter (*centi-* means one one-hundredth) is the unit for smaller lengths. The gram is the unit for weight, but

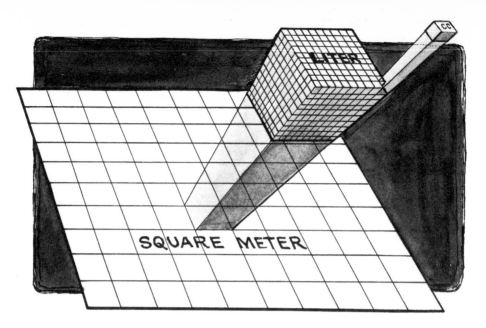

the kilogram is used to measure larger weights (masses).

To measure volume — milk, gasoline, strawberries, that sort of thing — a liter was used. This was a container 1 decimeter (10 centimeters) in each dimension.

The entire system was based on the meter — a square meter for area, a cubic centimeter (cc) for mass, or weight at sea level, a cubic decimeter for volume. A larger unit for measuring volume was the stere. This was a cube one meter in each dimension.

The metric system proposed in 1791 was precise. It was very easy to change one unit to another because the next higher unit was always 10 times the lower one: 10 millimeters equaled 1 centimeter, 10 centimeters equaled 1 decimeter, 10 decimeters equaled 1 meter. Also, a person did not have to remember different relationships for weight and

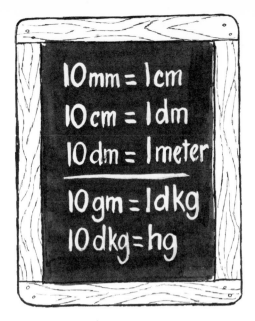

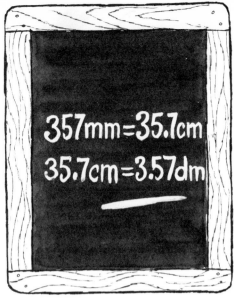

volume. In every case the next higher unit was 10 times the lower one. Ten grams equaled 1 decagram, 10 decagrams equaled 1 hectogram, and so on.

The units are easily manageable. For example, to change millimeters to centimeters all you do is divide by 10. And that's easy, just move the decimal point one place to the left, so 357 millimeters becomes 35.7 centimeters. Furthermore, if you wish to change centimeters to decimeters, all you do is divide by 10 again, or move the decimal another place to the left (35.7 centimeters becomes 3.57 decimeters).

Suppose on the other hand you wanted to change inches to feet, you'd have to divide by 12 (672 inches becomes 56 feet). If you wanted to change feet to yards, you'd divide by 3 (56 feet becomes 18 2/3 yards).

In the metric system you change larger units to

smaller ones by multiplying by 10. For example, 32 kilograms becomes 320 hectograms, and 320 hectograms becomes 3,200 decagrams, and so it goes.

Under the English system to change pounds to ounces you'd multiply by 16: 8 pounds would become 128 ounces; and to change to grains you'd have to multiply 128 by 437.5 (there are 437.5 grains in an ounce).

The metric system had many advantages over the diverse and haphazard units used in different countries. Even so, many decades went by before France accepted it. Most of the countries in the world gradually adopted the metric system, but America and the British Commonwealth of Nations—Great Britain, Canada, India, Australia, and many African nations— did not. This was probably because during the nineteenth century a thriving trade had been built between England and the United States, and England, especially, felt that if it changed the measuring system their profitable trade would be interrupted.

Trade between metric and nonmetric nations was awkward, and many mistakes were made. Lumber that was 3 meters long might be ordered, and when the shipment arrived the lumber might be 3 yards long— about 23 centimeters too short. Or wine might be priced by the quart or gallon in one country, and it would be bought and sold by the liter in another country. Scientists in nonmetric countries reading about

Le 20 mai 1875
L'Académie des Sciences
établit
Le Bureau International des Poids et Mesures

precise measurements in milligrams or milliliters had to change the measurements to ounces or fractions of inches. That caused a lot of confusion, so scientists all over the world—including the nonmetric nations—adopted the metric system almost from its inception.

But the people did not. So the confusion continued, except in scientific circles.

Finally, on May 20, 1875, the French Academy of Sciences, encouraged by other national groups, established the International Bureau of Weights and Measures. It was installed at Sèvres, France, just outside Paris. Three years later twenty nations around the world sent representatives to a General Conference on Weights and Measures. One of the first jobs of the members of the conference was to set new standards for the meter, gram, and liter. They wanted to get more precise and unchanging standards than those established in 1791.

The meter, which was still the standard for the whole system, was to be the distance between two finely engraved lines on a bar made of a mixture of platinum

26

and iridium—two hard, durable metals that expand and contract very little when heated or cooled. The distance was determined when the metal was at the freezing temperature of water. This fixed temperature —the freezing point of pure water—is often used to standardize measurements of materials that expand when heated, contract when cooled. The length of the new meter was very close to the original meter— 1/10,000,000 of the distance from the equator to the pole.

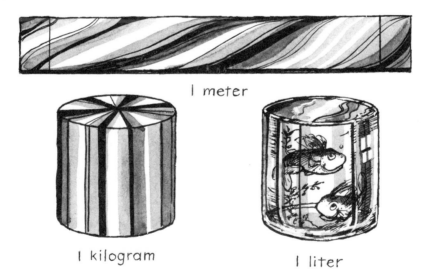

1 meter

1 kilogram

1 liter

At about the same time, the kilogram was defined as the mass, or weight at sea level, of a particular metal cylinder. Copies of the cylinder were supplied to all nations that were members of the conference.

The liter was the volume occupied by a kilogram of pure water at a temperature of 39° F.

27

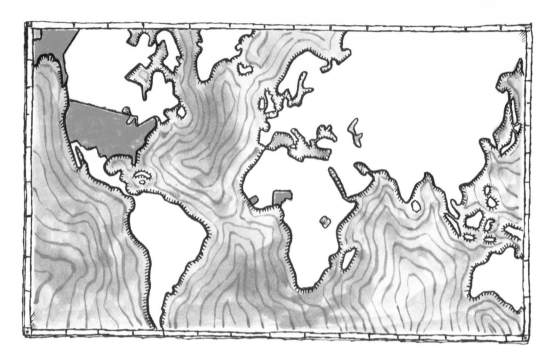

Some forty nations now belong to the Metric Convention, as it has come to be known. Every few years representatives meet to discuss improvements in the system—ways to make it more precise, and to make it more easily usable.

Since 1875 almost the entire world has adopted the metric system. England's date for dropping the English system of feet, pounds, quarts, and bushels, and going on the metric system is 1975. The map shows that only the United States and a few African states—Nigeria and Sierra Leone among them—will still be using the English system of measurements.

The General Conference on Weights and Measures held in 1960 again adopted new standards for the

meter and other units. Many additional nations had joined the group, because they realized the need for a system of standard measurements. The standards are essentially the same as the former units, but the chances for error have been reduced because our ability to set precise standards has increased. With the growth of precision machinery, rocket engines, and sophisticated spacecraft, the need for better measurements became greater.

The new system which, hopefully, will be adopted throughout the world is called the International System of Units. It is usually abbreviated SI, for the French, Système International. The system does not change the standards used under the metric system. It makes them more precise, more unchanging. Under the metric system the international meter was kept in Sèvres, France. Each country that belonged to the Metric Convention had a copy of that meter. Every few years they would have to check their copy against the international standard.

But the SI meter can be checked at any well-equipped science laboratory anywhere in the world. Although the new meter is the same length as it was in the metric system, the standard is based upon measurement of the wavelength of light. When a substance is heated, it gives off light. The light travels in waves. The length of these waves, which is always the same, can be measured. It was found that 1,650,763.73 wavelengths of the orange-red light of the heated gas krypton equaled a metric meter. Therefore this is now the standard for all the world. Anyone with the proper equipment can check the length of the meter with great accuracy.

The metal meter bars deposited in each of the

Tube with krypton gas

several countries will not be discarded. They will be used, as in the past, for day to day use and for checking various measuring devices. But when the most accurate measurements are required the standard mentioned above will be used. The meter is the basis for measuring area; the size of a lot, a floor, or a tabletop. It is also the basis for measuring the volume of a container.

Under SI the unit of mass, or weight at sea level, is the kilogram. The standard is no different from that used in the metric system and adopted at the end of the last century: the mass of a metal cylinder made of platinum and iridium. The weight of the cylinder is very nearly the same as the weight of 1,000 cc. (cubic centimeters) of water at 39° F. This would be the amount of water in a cube 10 centimeters on each side.

Under SI a reliable, unchanging standard was established for measuring time. We have not mentioned time before because the standard for measuring it has been widely accepted. There has been no problem of matching a metric second, let us say, with an English second.

The basis for time-keeping for many centuries has been the rotation of the earth on its axis; and the revolution of the earth around the sun. These are events that occur regularly year in and year out, and so have served quite well as clocks. However, the earth does not always rotate at exactly the same speed; it is slightly fast at times, slightly slow at other times. So also with the movement of the earth about the sun.

At the meeting of the General Conference on Weights and Measures held in 1960 it was decided that the second, the unit of time, should be 1/31,556,-925.9747 of the year 1900. This is certainly a tiny fraction and should be accurate, but because of variations in years, it was decided that a more precise, regular, and readily measurable standard should be found.

In 1967 it was decided to use an atomic clock. Radioactive elements give off radiation at a fixed rate. The best atomic measure for the second has turned out to be the time required for the cesium atom to give off 9,192,630,770 cycles of radiation. Now it is possible for any physics laboratory equipped with the proper apparatus to determine the second, as it is accepted around the world.

SI takes care of temperature measurements, too. The Fahrenheit scale discussed earlier was rejected. Not long after Fahrenheit set his standards for measuring temperature, it was discovered that 0° F. was not the coldest possible temperature. This meant that minus readings on the Fahrenheit scale had no useful meaning. They were simply readings lower than Fahrenheit reached with his salt-ice mixture.

In 1742, Anders Celsius, a Swedish scientist, devised a different scaling for his thermometer. It was based on a hundred steps, and so was called the centigrade scale. (*Centum* is a Latin word meaning "hundred," and *gradus* means "degree.") Celsius decided that the freezing point of water should be 0° and the boiling point 100°. He had a hundred divisions between freezing and boiling. The Fahrenheit thermometer had 180°. Minus readings on Celsius' scale meant below the freezing point of water.

We now know that much colder temperatures than 0° F. (the temperature Fahrenheit believed was the coldest of all) can be reached. We believe the coldest temperature is −459° F., or −273.15° C. (C for Celsius). It is called absolute zero.

In both the Fahrenheit and centigrade (properly called Celsius) scales temperatures are read as minus quantities as they become colder. Lord Kelvin, an outstanding English scientist, suggested in 1848 that this was not right. Temperature is something, he said, and so no matter what the temperature may be, the reading should always be plus. Only when all the heat is taken from a substance can its temperature be zero, he said. He called it absolute zero. There can never be a minus reading on Kelvin's scale. He determined that absolute zero would be the bottom of his scale. Then he applied the Celsius scale. The freezing point of water would be +273.15, or 273.15° K., he said (K for Kelvin, or sometimes you might see A, A for absolute). The boiling point of water in this system is 373.15° K. — one hundred degrees above freezing.

The Kelvin system of measuring temperature is retained by SI. Hopefully it will rapidly gain acceptance around the world because, as Kelvin argued, tempera-

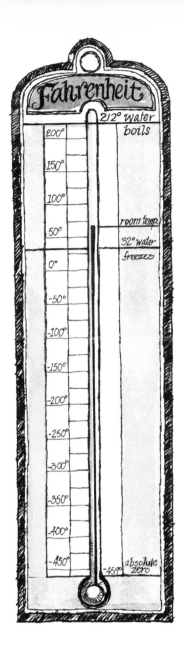

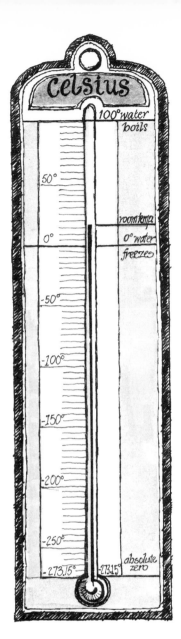

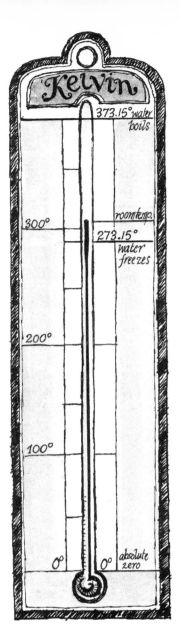

ture is real and there should be no such thing as a minus temperature reading.

A look at the various measuring units listed on pages 46, 47, 48, and 49 shows the variety that existed

around the world and the difficulty that arose when one unit was compared with another.

The SI standards are simple and they are the result of refinements that have come about because of man's concern with measurement through many centuries.

When metric is used (and it probably will become truly international by 1980) you will buy liquids (milk, gasoline, fruit juices) by the liter or fractions of a liter. You'll give your weight in kilograms and your height in meters.

At first it sounds strange. But once you start using metric you'll get used to it rapidly. You can start by following these directions. You'll need cardboard and scissors.

1	2	3	4	5	6	7	8	9	10

This strip is 1 decimeter (10 centimeters) long. When you think metric you would not ordinarily use the word decimeter. Although you know the strip is a decimeter long, you would call it 10 centimeters. This is the terminology used by people in European countries.

Lay a strip of cardboard along it. Then mark the cardboard as we have done. Divide it into 10 parts — each one is a centimeter.

Get a long piece of cardboard; a stick would be better. Using your 10-centimeter strip, mark off 10 decimeters and also 100 centimeters. This will give you a meter stick.

You can use your meter stick to make large

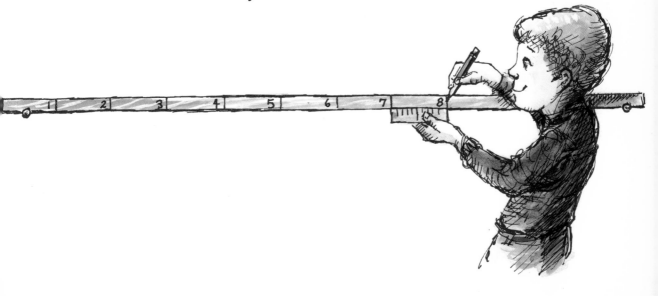

measurements and your 10-centimeter strip of card-board to make smaller ones.

Measure a table as we did. We got 1.2 meters by 80 centimeters (.8 meters). To find square meters in the surface of the table all we had to do was multiply 1.2 × .8 and that gave us .96 square meters.

Suppose we were measuring another table in the English system, and the dimensions turned out to be 1 yard 2 feet 3 inches by 2 feet 7 inches. To find the number of square feet in the tabletop we would have to multiply 5 1/4 feet by 2 7/12 feet; or, changing the dimensions to inches, multiply 63 inches by 31 inches and divide the answer by 144 because there are 144 square inches in 1 square foot.

It's quite obvious that metric is much easier to handle. To give you some idea of the metric dimensions of things around you, try the following:

Find the height of the ceiling in meters.

Find the length, width, and thickness of this book in centimeters.

How long is your father's car?

How big is your kitchen? How many square meters?

Measure the size of your bed. How many square meters in it?

How tall are you, your sisters and brothers, your father and mother, in meters, in centimeters, in millimeters?

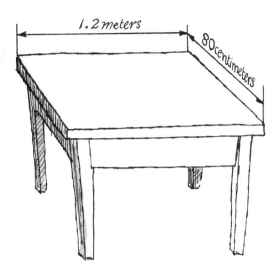

1.2 meters

80 centimeters

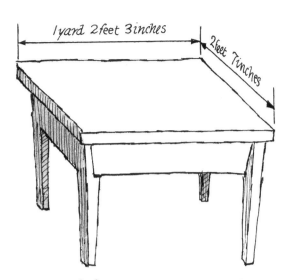

1 yard 2 feet 3 inches

2 feet 7 inches

1.2 × .8 = .96 square meters

5¼ feet × 2½ feet
or
63" × 31" = 1953 square inches
1953 ÷ 144 = 13 81/144 square feet

One thousand meters make a kilometer. This is the unit used for measuring larger distances. Instead of saying it's so many miles from one place to another, for example, you would say it's so many kilometers.

It is about 4,800 kilometers from New York to California.

The diameter of the earth is about 12,800 kilometers.

The distance to the moon is about 387,000 kilometers.

> How far in kilometers is it to the nearest big city? to the sun?
>
> What is the diameter in kilometers of the moon? the sun? Mercury? Mars?

Under metric the unit for measuring volume is the cubic meter. That would be a cube, or box, 1 meter in each dimension.

Liquids are usually measured in liters. That's 1/1,000 of a cubic meter. You can make a liter box as follows: Using your cardboard decimeter (10 centimeters), cut out five pieces of cardboard, each 10 centimeters square. On both sides of four of the squares mark the level of 2.5, 5, and 7.5 centimeters. These will be the sides of your liter box. Tape the pieces together to make a box with gradations all around the inside and outside. The box is 1 liter, or 1,000 cubic centimeters, or 1 cubic decimeter.

40

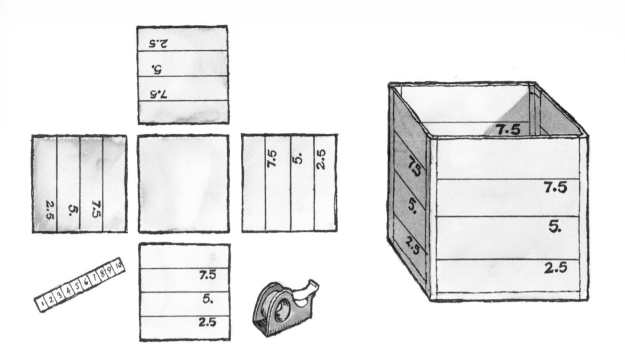

What part of a liter is a pound of rice?
What part of a liter is a 2-lb. box of sugar?
What part of a liter is a pound of ground coffee?

Because your liter box is not waterproof, to find liter equivalents of glasses, cups, and bottles use sand or sugar in place of liquids. Using sand or sugar find:

What part of a liter is the glass you ordinarily use for milk?
What part of a liter does a bottle of soda hold?
What part of a liter does a coffee cup hold?

You could make a waterproof liter box using waterproof glue and plastic sheets thin enough to cut with scissors but heavy enough to make a measuring box. Both are available at most hardware stores. Then you could measure liquids directly.

The meter, the basic unit for length measures under metric, is the basis for measuring volume and also, in a way, it is the basis for measuring mass, or sea-level weight.

The liter box, 10 centimeters on each side, contains 1,000 cubic centimeters. If it were filled with water, and the water were 4° C. (277° K.), the water would weigh just about 1,000 grams (1 kilogram). One cubic centimeter (1 cc) of water weighs just about 1 gram (1 g).

A pound equals about .45 kilograms. Knowing this, figure out:

How much you weigh in kilograms.
How much your mother weighs, your father, brother, sister.
How much your dog weighs in kilograms.
A box of sugar.
A bag of apples.
A bag of potatoes.

The metric system (or SI) is fun. Measurements of distance, mass, and volume are made using only meters and centimeters, grams, kilograms, and liters.

Think metric. Pretty soon everyone will. Only the United States and a few other countries are still using the obsolete English system.

Sooner or later the United States will be using Système International. Our road signs will be changed, our rulers, shoe and dress sizes, our cans and bottles —everything will be metric, so—

Think metric. Pretty soon that's the way the whole world will be thinking.

HOW UNITS IN THE METRIC SYSTEM ARE CHANGED
FROM ONE TO THE OTHER

Units within the box are those most frequently used. To change from one to another, multiply or divide by ten.

PREFIX	SYM-BOL	POWER		EXAMPLE
(meters, grams, liters)				
tera	T	10^{12}	1,000,000,000,000	
giga	G	10^{9}	1,000,000,000	
mega	M	10^{6}	1,000,000	megawatts
kilo	k	10^{3}	1,000	kilometer
hecto	h	10^{2}	100	hectometer
deca	da	10^{1}	10	decagram
1 meter, 1 gram, 1 liter			1	
deci	d	10^{-1}	.1	decigram
centi	c	10^{-2}	.01	centiliter
milli	m	10^{-3}	.001	millimeter
micro	u	10^{-6}	.000001	microsecond
nano	n	10^{-9}	.000000001	
pico	p	10^{-12}	.000000000001	
femto	f	10^{-15}	.000000000000001	
atto	a	10^{-18}	.000000000000000001	

Here we see the simplicity of relationships under SI. Ten milli (meters, grams, liters) equals 1 centi, 10 centis equals 1 deci, 10 decis equals 1. And continuing, 10 (meters, grams, liters) equals 1 deca, 10 decas equals 1 hecto, and 10 hectos gives 1 kilo. To go from larger to smaller units all you need to do is move the decimal point one place to the right—add zeros. One kilogram equals 10 hectograms, equals 100 decagrams, equals 1,000 grams, equals 10,000 decigrams, and so it goes.

ENGLISH–METRIC EQUIVALENTS

Including current and obsolete units. Those in bold type are current.

UNIT	ENGLISH	METRIC
acre	= 43,560 sq. ft.	40.4686 ares
angstrom	= 0.000000004 in.	0.0001 micron
are	= 119.6 sq. yds.	100 m^2
	= .02471 acres	
barleycorn	= 1/3 in.	8.5 mm
barn gallon	= 2.40 gals.	9.09 l
barrel (fruits)	= 7,056 cu. in.	115.62 l
barrel (oil)	= 42 gals.	158.98 l
bodge	= 1/2 peck	
bolt (cloth)	= 40 yds.	36.58 m
bolt (wallpaper)	= 16 yds.	14.63 m
bushel	= 32 qts.	35.23 l
cable	= 120 fathoms	219.456 m
carat	= 3.086 g.	200 mg
centiare	= 1.196 sq. yds.	
centiliter	= .338 fl. oz.	.01 l
centimeter	= 0.3937 in.	
centistere	= .353 cu. ft.	.01 m^3
chain	= 22 yds.	20.12 m
chain	= 0.10 acre	4.047 ares
chalder	= 37.15 bu.	13.09 hl
coomb	= 4.13 bu.	145.7 l
cord	= 128 cu. ft.	
cranne (herring)	= 45 gals.	170.3 l
cubic centimeter	= 0.061 cu. in.	
cubic decimeter	= 61.023 cu. in.	
cubic foot	=	28.317 dm^3
cubic inch	=	16.387 cm^3
cubic meter	= 1.31 cu. yds.	
cubic yard	=	0.76 m^3
cup	= 8 fl. oz.	
decaliter	= 610.25 cu. in.	
decameter	= 32.808 ft.	

46

ENGLISH–METRIC EQUIVALENTS (continued)

UNIT	ENGLISH	METRIC
decare	= 0.2471 acre	
decastere	= 13.08 cu. yd.	
decimeter	= 3.937 in.	
digit	= .75 in.	1.905 cm
dram (apothecaries')	= 60 grains	3.888 g
dram (fl.)	= 0.226 cu. in.	3.697 ml
drum	= 50–55 gals.	
fathom	= 6 ft.	1.829 m
firkin	= 10.8 gals.	40.91 l
foot	= 12 in., 1/3 yd.	0.305 m
furlong	= 660 ft., 220 yds.	201.168 m
gallon (U.S.)	= 128 fl. oz.	3.785 l
gallon (Eng.)	= 160 Brit. oz.	4.546 l
gill	= 4 fl. oz.	0.118 l
goad	= 4 1/2 ft.	1.37 m
grain	=	64.799 mg
gram	= 15.432 grains	
hand	= 4 in.	10.16 cm
hectare	= 2.471 acres	10,000 m^2
		100 ares
hectoliter	= 26.418 gals.	
hectostere	= 130.8 cu. yds.	100 m^3
hundredweight (long)	= 112 lbs.	50.802 kg
hundredweight (short)	= 100 lbs.	45.359 kg
inch	= 1/12 ft., 1.36 yds.	2.54 cm
kilogram	= 2.20 lbs.	1,000 g
kiloliter	= 35.315 cu. ft.	1,000 l
kilometer	= 0.621 mi.	
league	= 3 mi.	4,828 km
line	= 0.0833 in.	2.12 mm
link	= 7.92 in.	0.201 m
liter	= 1.06 qts.	
meter	= 39.37 in., 1.094 yds., 3.281 ft.	
meter (cube)	= 1.308 cu. yds.	
meter (square)	= 1.196 sq. yds.	

ENGLISH–METRIC EQUIVALENTS (continued)

UNIT	ENGLISH	METRIC
microgram	=	0.000001 g
micron	= 0.00003937 in.	0.001 mm
mil	= 0.001 in.	0.0254 mm
mile	= 5,280 ft., 1,760 yds.	1.610 km
mile (statute)	= 5,280 ft.	1.609 km
mile (nautical)	= 6,080.20 ft.	1.853 km
mile (square)	= 640 acres	
milligram	= 0.015 grain	
milliliter	= 0.271 fl. dram	
millimeter	= 0.0394 (1/25) in.	
millimicron	= 0.00000003937 in.	0.001 micron
minim	= 1/60 fl. dram	
ounce	= 437.5 grains	28.350 g
ounce (fl.)	= 1/16 pt.	
ounce (Troy)	= 480 grains	
palm	= 3 or 4 in.	7.62 or 10.16 cm
peck	= 8 qts.	8.810 l
pennyweight	= 24 grains	1.555 g
perch (U.S.)	= 1 rod	5.029 m
perch (Eng.)	= 30 1/4 sq. yds.	25.29 m^2
pin	= 5.4 gals.	20.46 l
pint (U.S.)	= 1/64 bu.	
pint (U.S.)	= 1/8 gal.	
pint (Eng.)	= 1.2 U.S. pts.	
point	= 0.01 carat	2 mg
pole	= 5 1/2 yds.	5.029 m
pound	= 5,760 grains	0.454 kg
puncheon	= 84 gals.	318 l
quart	= 1/4 gal.	0.951 l
quart	= 1/32 bu.	1.101 l
quarter (mile)	= 440 yds.	402.34 m
rod (pole, perch)	= 16 1/2 ft., 5 1/2 yds.	5.029 m
rood	= 40 sq. yds., 1/4 acre	

UNIT	ENGLISH	METRIC
rundlet	= 18 gals.	68 l
scruple	= 20 grains	1.296 g
square (shingles)	= 100 sq. ft.	
square centimeter (cm^2)	= 0.155 sq. in.	
square decimeter (dm^2)	= 15.500 sq. in.	
square foot (sq. ft.)	=	929.034 cm^2
square inch	=	6.452 cm^2
square kilometer (km^2)	= 247.104 acres, 0.386 sq. mi.	
square meter	= 1.196 sq. yds., 10.764 sq. ft.	
square mile	=	259 hectares
square millimeter (mm^2)	= 0.002 sq. in.	
square rod, pole, perch	=	25.293 m^2
square yard	=	0.836 m^2
stack	= 108 cu. ft.	3.06 m^3
stere	= 1.308 cu. yds.	1 m^3
stone	= 14 lbs.	
strike	= 4 bu.	145.5 l
tablespoon	= 3 tsps., 4 fl. drams	
teaspoon	= 1 1/3 fl. drams	
tierce	= 42 wine gals.	159 l
ton (Eng.)	= 2,240 lbs.	
ton (long)	= 2,240 lbs.	1,000 kg
ton (short)	= 2,000 lbs.	
township	= 36 sq. mi.	9,324 hectares
tub (oysters)	= 3 bu.	1.06 hl
tun	= 252 wine gals.	953.9 l
yard	= 3 ft., 36 in.	0.914 m

INDEX

ABOUT THE AUTHOR

Dr. Franklyn M. Branley is well known as the author of many excellent science books for young people of all ages. He is also co-editor of the Let's-Read-and-Find-Out science books.

Dr. Branley is Astronomer and Chairman of the American Museum-Hayden Planetarium in New York City.

He holds degrees from New York University, Columbia University, and the State University of New York College at New Paltz. He lives with his family in Woodcliff Lake, New Jersey.

ABOUT THE ARTIST

Graham Booth was born in London but grew up in Victoria, British Columbia. He was graduated from UCLA and received his master's degree in fine arts from the University of Southern California. Mr. Booth—author, designer, and active lecturer on the illustration of children's books—has appeared on numerous panels concerned with children's literature and has received many awards for his work. He presently teaches art at Fullerton Junior College.

Graham Booth lives in Laguna Beach, California, with his wife and two young sons. They summer on an island off the coast of British Columbia, where Mr. Booth paints and scuba dives for relaxation.